A GUIDE ON HOW TO CREATE NEW BEGINNINGS BY
PEELING OFF OBSTACLES IN LIFE.

PEELING OFF THE
LAYERS TO UNMASK

New Beginnings

STACEY DORI GAREL

*This book is dedicated to God for his many blessings and protection.
To my beautiful late grandmother Pearline Stinson for being my
heavenly angel,
and for prophesying this opportunity to me. To my loving mother
Beverly Stinson & family,
who have always believed in me,
supported my dreams,
and encouraged my creativity.*

*You have been my guiding light,
my source of strength,
and my constant inspiration.
Thank you for your unwavering love,
and for always being there for me.*

*This book is dedicated to you,
for being the foundation of my success,
and for being the reason I never gave up.
I am forever grateful for your love and support.*

*With all my heart,
Stacey "Dori" Garel*

Table of Contents

Introduction

In a world where we often find ourselves defined by the masks we wear, "Peeling Off the Layers to Unmask New Beginnings" invites you on a profound exploration of personal growth and self-discovery. This transformative book takes you on a captivating journey of peeling away the layers that conceal our true selves, unveiling the limitless potential and authentic essence that lie beneath.

Through poignant stories, insightful reflections, and practical guidance, this book delves deep into Stacey Dori's experiences, encouraging readers to embrace vulnerability and let go of the past. With each layer shed, a new beginning emerges, filled with possibility, purpose, and the freedom to live life authentically.

Drawing from personal encounters, spirituality, and the wisdom of obstacles Stacey Dori embarked on through her own transformative journeys, "Peeling Off the Layers to Unmask New Beginnings" offers a roadmap to uncovering your true self. It explores the power of self-acceptance, self-love, and the courage to let go of societal expectations, allowing you to step into your true potential and create a life that aligns with your deepest desires.

Whether you're seeking personal growth, healing, or a fresh start, this book serves as a guiding light, reminding us that true liberation lies in the willingness to peel off the layers of conditioning, fear, and self-doubt. It empowers you to embrace change, embrace your authentic self, and embrace the infinite possibilities that await you on the other side of unmasking new beginnings.

Are you ready to embark on a journey of self-discovery, peel off the layers, and unleash the power within? Join us as we delve into the transformative journey of "Peeling Off the Layers to Unmask New Beginnings."

CHAPTER 1

Self-love Discovery

My Story

If you have ever questioned your worth, this is for you. Many times in life, we lose sight of who we are. You may find it hard to separate yourself from the things you see others either accomplish or experience. You must understand that everyone has their own unique path that they must follow. In this chapter, I will explain how I peeled off the barrier preventing me from loving myself. In discovering how to love ourselves, we often limit our ability to look deeper to see the greatness within. At times we allow others to control the narrative of who we are by accepting what they think, say, or how they treat us versus finding a sense of self. When we lose sight of ourselves, we silence our own voice and inner strength.

Let us first describe what self-love encompasses. Self-love discovery is understanding what you truly desire, your thoughts (remember, your thoughts can hinder your elevation), your goals, and what inspires you. As you set out on the journey and discovery of self-love, know that it is not an overnight process. While discovering your power and purpose, learn that all great things take time and obedience. Allow yourself to pace yourself and create a routine that works best for you. Take time to reflect on the things you want to peel away from your life and release all that no longer serves a place in your life.

My breakthrough to finally embracing self-love, my challenges with loving myself, and identifying how to love myself first began at a very early age. I can remember the first feeling of abandoning energy. It was when my father departed our home when I was about two years of age. I can recall him telling my older sister and me that he would be back and walking out the door, never to come back. There were times during that period of my life when my sister and I would pack our bags and wait all day and night until the sun faded, sitting in the window, looking out for him to show up on the promise of coming back to pick us up. Falling asleep still sitting by the window; waking up as he never showed.

By the time I was four, I remember telling my sister in a very angry voice, "He is not coming back," throwing my bag down, running into my room, and yelling "Why doesn't my dad love me?" I was blaming myself for my dad's inability to embrace fatherhood. At this time, I realized that my father was the first man to break my heart. The effect of this heartbreak would take a toll on me so strongly that I found myself in childhood depression. I became so cold-hearted and angry. I shut off from the world, isolated myself, and created my own inner happiness through writing poems in a journal. This was the only thing that brought me joy. Writing had become my way of getting my feelings out of my subconscious mind to feel free.

During my childhood years, I experienced some hurt and

challenges that a child should never have had to experience. This was another situation of being silenced. This event made me emptier inside, took my voice away completely, and gave me a fear of being vulnerable around men. I can recall during this time in life being bullied because I didn't talk much, and I was often teased by other kids in elementary school because of my very light-skinned complexion and fine hair. Fitting in for me was not an option as I had to turn to my outer strength for protection. At that point, I began to take my power and fight back, not with words but physically. I recall the first time I had to use my hands instead of my words, at the age of eleven years old, when I was being chased down the hall by a group of girls with scissors attempting to cut my hair because they said I had hair that a melanated girl should not have. They held me down and brought the scissors close to my hair, attempting to cut each lock of my hair off. I closed my eyes and blacked out for a moment in fear, but at that moment, I had awakened something strong inside of me, a force so strong that I pushed them off me and began fighting back until each one had run off crying. This soon became the power I felt I needed to protect myself; however, it was just another setback as I didn't want to go through life angry and feeling as if my only way of protecting myself was to be physical.

However, the bullying became worse throughout my years in elementary school. During this period of my life, I had glasses and braces to correct my smile and straighten my teeth. As I worked on my minor imperfections, I was told I was ugly, called numerous names, and felt left out. I found myself alone most of the time, quiet in every room I was in, and not learning how to love myself. After a few more years during my developmental stage, my braces had come off and my mother allowed me to get contacts during our winter break in high school. This was my first time ever looking in the mirror and feeling beautiful. As a gift for getting my braces off, my orthodontist had given me a free photoshoot to show off my smile. Embracing this opportunity, I felt free and beautiful. I went back to school from this break and stood by my locker, observing several guys walking by and asking who the new girl was. I remember looking around trying to see who they were referring to only to find out they were talking about me. Finally, I felt accepted by my peers and built new friendships and my first high school relationship.

After high school, my passion for all things beauty and glam led me to beauty pageants, acting, and modeling. I was at the height of my career when I met and fell in love with my ex-fiancé. We were together for ten years. In the first two years, things were amazing and we were inseparable. We took trips together, he made me feel beautiful, loved, and needed. It wasn't until year four that our relationship began to shift. He had become very controlling and emotionally abusive. He would tell me that I was lucky to have him and that no other man would want or love me. I loved this man so much that I believed every word he said. We eventually moved in together, thinking this would bring our relationship more stability, only for me to become a prisoner in my own home. Whenever his friends would come over, he would lock me in the bedroom for hours while he entertained his company. I would be in our room with no food or access to the bathroom for hours. After his friends left, he would let me out of the room to an empty fridge, messy kitchen, and dirty bathroom. I would then need to clean and restock the fridge.

By year nine into this relationship, I began to find the strength to exit. I had come home early from work one day and noticed things in our bedroom that did not belong to me and overheard him talking to a female on the phone. I confronted him about it, and he admitted to infidelity. I grabbed my keys and ran to my car in tears. I went back to my mother's home and stayed with her for a day. The following day he asked if he could come by to talk. I agreed, and once he came over, our discussion became heated, and I told him to leave. I walked him out of the garage area and walked away from him as he was yelling at me. He came up to me as my back was turned to him and called out my name. I turned around and said, "Yes?" Once I turned around, he smacked me hard across my face with a force so strong that my 120-pound body hit the wall in the garage room, causing me to blackout. As I started to regain consciousness, I heard him on the phone with a friend of his saying he thought he killed his girl. His friend told him to check if I was breathing. I saw him walking in my direction and I began to play dead as I feared what he might do next. At that moment, he walked up to my body and kicked me with force, telling his friend I wasn't moving. His friend then instructed him to leave. Once I saw him head towards the door, I began to get up to get help. My head was hurting so badly, and blood began to pour from the back of my head. He heard me get up and ran over to me, pinning me back down on the ground. I pleaded with him to let go, and he refused as he feared he would be arrested. I told him I wouldn't call the police and to let me get help. As I pleaded, his grip got tighter and I knew in that moment that I had to go back to using my physical strength. I pushed him off and ran into the house.

The commotion was so loud that my mother came downstairs to ask what was going on. Once she saw me, she started screaming "What did you do to my daughter?!" as my shirt was covered with blood. She called for assistance, and I was placed into an ambulance and taken to the hospital. I was evaluated and told I had a concussion, a cracked skull, and a dislocated shoulder. I was asked several times by hospital staff and police if someone had done this. I lied and said no to protect him and feared that he would retaliate.

During this incident, I had to go through physical therapy as I had no feeling in my right shoulder or hand. I basically had to teach myself how to write all over again. For months he called me, begging me to take him back, and that he made a mistake. Promising it would never happen again. I took him back and he proposed. I was so excited about our next steps; however, the relationship was done. He would show me more signs of infidelity and abuse. In year ten, I completely walked away and let go of my fears. Loving myself allowed room for growth and healing. I knew that all I ever needed was to love myself and let go of my self-doubt.

Remember, embracing self-love can cultivate a positive mindset. Be patient with yourself, celebrate your progress, and don't allow more setbacks. You are about to enjoy a beautiful journey of self-discovery and growth. Embrace it wholeheartedly and allow the love and positivity within you to radiate outward, transforming your life and the lives of those around you.

Through all the challenging experiences you have experienced, the exercises outlined in this chapter will help you peel away the layers of self-doubt, fear, and insecurity that have held you back from realizing your true potential. Along the way, you will learn to appreciate your unique strengths and embrace your flaws, ultimately discovering a newfound sense of self-love and acceptance. Explore the complexities of self-discovery and the power of love to transform your life. Once you understand who you are, you will open new doors of endless possibilities by activating your superpower. Regaining the power to stand strong within and allowing you to show up for you!

Peeling Off the Layers

Start and end your day with gratitude: Take a moment to express gratitude for another day in life and all the wonderful things you have accomplished thus far. Before you go to bed each night, reflect on the positive moments of your day. This practice helps shift your focus toward appreciation and sets a positive tone for productive days ahead.

Self-love is also discovering self-care: You know the old saying "You are what you eat"? Nourish your mind and body with healthy foods and drink plenty of water. Take care of yourself holistically by prioritizing your health. Remember, health is wealth! A healthy body creates and helps you generate your networking skills to produce your net worth. Find meditation activities that you enjoy and that bring inner peace, such as creating a hobby, going for a walk in nature, practicing yoga, or listening to uplifting music.

Embrace self-compassion: Treat yourself with the same kindness and compassion you would extend to others. When faced with challenges, remind yourself that it is okay to make mistakes.

Set healthy boundaries: Put your own needs first. Learn to say "no" when necessary, and do not feel guilty for taking time for yourself. Prioritize self-care and ensure that your emotional and mental well-being are not compromised.

Challenge negative self-talk: Pay attention to the conversations you participate in. Even though the tea is hot, it does not mean you have to drink it. Engaging in negative conversations only allows negative energy to consume your energy and can stagnate your progress.

Surround yourself with positivity: Surround yourself with people who uplift and support you. Seek out relationships that are nurturing and inspire personal growth. Additionally, be mindful of the media and information you consume. Choose content that aligns with your values, inspires you, and promotes positivity.

Next Steps

I want to give you some next steps in your discovery. Let's start with some grounding meditations. Grounding is a type of meditation that helps put you back in touch with the present moment by focusing attention on the physical world around you. You can use grounding meditation by placing your bare feet into the grass or dirt of the Earth or by sitting on a chair with your feet set flat on the ground. You may also lay flat on the ground, grass, sand, or by submerging yourself in water.

Once you are in a position to ground, I want you to take a deep breath and close your eyes. Try to block out all the harsh words you have heard throughout your life, all the heartbreak, feelings of not being good enough, or self-doubt. Let go of the pain as you are now entering into your new season of elevation. You are about to reclaim your worth, the value you bring to the world, and your inner strength.

Slowly, begin to let go of the insults and negativity that have burdened you for so long. Now, open your eyes and stand up. You are now feeling empowered and ready to start fresh. It is time to start walking towards your purpose. Be determined to make a brighter future for yourself.

As you walk towards your purpose, you will start to feel the hurt and the pain that has been weighing you down finally start to peel away. Look up at the sky and accept the sense of peace that shines over you as it radiates throughout your body. Embrace your inner and outer beauty! You are no longer able to let any negativity define your life. Find your strength and reassurance so that you can choose a brighter future. You are capable of great things, and you can create a brighter future.

Adjust your crown, walk in your purpose with courage and conviction, love yourself, and believe in your own power. Embrace these affirmations daily, repeating them aloud or writing them down. Let them sink into your subconscious mind and guide your thoughts towards self-confidence and self-worth. Remember, you are deserving of all the love and greatness that life has to offer. You are now on track! No more looking back.

1. I am worthy of love, happiness, and success.
2. I embrace my uniqueness and celebrate my individuality.
3. I am deserving of all the good that comes into my life.

4. I radiate confidence and attract positive energy.
5. I let go of negative self-talk and embrace self-compassion.
6. I am enough, just as I am, and I accept myself wholly.
7. I can overcome any challenges that come my way.
8. I trust my instincts and make decisions that align with my values.
9. I am resilient and bounce back from setbacks stronger than before.
10. I believe in my abilities and have faith in my dreams.
11. I release comparisons and focus on my own growth and success.
12. I am surrounded by love, support, and uplifting relationships.
13. I am in control of my thoughts, and I choose positivity.
14. I honor my needs and take care of my mental, emotional, and physical well-being.
15. I embrace new opportunities with enthusiasm and confidence.
16. I am constantly evolving and growing into the best version of myself.
17. I deserve happiness and allow myself to experience joy fully.
18. I trust that the universe is working in my favor, bringing me abundance.
19. I am grateful for all that I am and all that I have accomplished.
20. I love and accept myself unconditionally, just as I am.

By embracing self-love and cultivating a positive mindset, you will unlock your potential for transformative change within your life. The tips outlined in this chapter are not a quick fix but a process to guide you along your ongoing journey of growth and self-discovery; it will take time and dedication. A solid foundation of self-love and positivity allows you to grow mentally, be resilient, decrease stress, and improve your overall health. Embark on this journey by embracing your worth, and create a life filled with love, joy, and possibility. Remember, you hold the power to shape your own happiness and mental well-being, so embrace it with open arms.

CHAPTER 2

Dealing with Grief

My Grief

Dealing with grief can be an incredibly challenging and personal journey. The first thing to always remember when grieving is to allow yourself to grieve. It's important to give yourself permission to feel and express your emotions. Allow yourself to cry, scream, or simply sit with your feelings. Recognize that grief is a natural response to loss and that it takes time to heal. Seek support. Surround yourself with a supportive network of friends, family, or support groups who can provide comfort and understanding. It's helpful when you share your thoughts and feelings with others who have experienced similar losses. It can be immensely helpful.

Losing someone in life is never easy. Getting that phone call, text message, or seeing a post on social media about a loved one passing can make you feel so empty inside as if you lost a part of yourself. In my life, I dealt with so many losses that have impacted me in ways I never would've imagined. At the age of sixteen, I lost my maternal aunt. She had come to our home to get assistance from my grandmother during her battle with cancer as it had resurfaced yet again; however, this time she knew in her heart that this would not go the way it had before. During her short time with us, she told my mother that she wanted to go shopping and do something special for everyone. We spent the whole day at the stores, and I remember looking at a pair of sandals that were trendy and very expensive at the time.

My aunt walked over to me and said, "Those would look nice on you." I tried them on and fell in love with the fit and look. She told me to take them off and place them back in the box. I did just that. She grabbed the box, took it to the register, and checked out. I was so thankful and happy that I wore them to school the following day. Once I got home from school, I ran up the stairs to see my aunt to tell her how much the kids at school loved my new shoes. Once I got to the top of the stairs, I saw her sitting on the edge of the bed coughing. I ran into the room to see if she needed anything, only to see the napkin in her hand over her mouth filled with blood. She looked at me very nervously and said go get your mother. I ran down the hall to my mother's room and got her and my grandmother. My grandmother came into the room, and she started praying and crying asking God to come into the room.

At that very moment, it was as if the room began to shake, and the lights began to flicker. The anointing was in the presence, and my grandmother began to speak in tongues and praise the Lord. My mother and I joined in, and I remember holding onto my aunt's hand. Her grip was so loose and weak that her hand slipped from mine as she began to look as if she was about to pass out. She then told my mother to take her to the hospital. At that very moment, it would be the last time my aunt came home. Over the next two days, my aunt was preparing everyone for her departure. She called each family member one by one into the room to say goodbye. When my turn was called, I walked into the hospital room.

She had a smile on her face and said to me, "Don't come in here with those big eyes of yours filled with tears. I'm ok, and I want you to make your mother proud and do something special for my daughter. Also, I want you to go to prom tomorrow night and enjoy it." She said, "I know you are going to look amazing." She told me that this would be her last time seeing me. I told her it wouldn't because my belief in God and his ability to change things would keep her here. She looked at me, smiled, and hugged me.

The next morning as I went to the hairdresser's to get prepared for prom, I saw one of my aunts coming into the shop to pick me up instead of my mother. I knew that something had happened. I remember jumping up out of the chair I was sitting in, running to my aunt, screaming "Please tell me she's still here!" My other aunt looked at me and shook her head no. This was the first time in my life I experienced grief where my soul felt empty inside. For years the pain of losing her took a toll on not only myself but my family as well. Especially my grandmother. She would always say that she was supposed to go before any of her children. I knew losing her firstborn child was one of the hardest things to experience in life. How do I know? Because I experienced that same pain in 2015.

2015 was supposed to be the best year for me. I had married my best friend, and we were expecting our first child. It was such a blessing to me, as I was told by a doctor at the age of sixteen that there may be a possibility I would not conceive any children in life. I was so excited; however, I didn't receive that same excitement from my husband. I can recall his response when we found out I was expecting, "I'm happy for you." I was confused at that moment. "Happy for me?" Not us? I didn't question his response as I wanted to remain stress-free, and I wanted to embrace all the joys of becoming a new mother.

I was already a wonderful stepmom to his four, beautiful daughters. For every doctor's appointment, my husband made excuses about why he could not attend, leaving me to either go alone or have my family step in. It was in month four of my pregnancy that things began to change for the worse. During this period of my pregnancy, I was working as a Tradeshow and Events Manager and was heading out of town for a conference when I decided to use the bathroom before my two-hour flight. As I began to go, I wiped, and as I wiped the tissue became filled with blood. I began to panic and got dressed, pacing swiftly to the departure counter to ask for assistance. Their team of staff immediately called for paramedics, and I was treated on the scene. The paramedics advised me to go to the hospital to get checked out. I called my husband, and he was back at the airport within ten minutes to take me. Once we got there, the hospital kept me in the waiting area for at least three hours. Nervously waiting, I began asking when someone would come out to check on me, and the medical team's response was always, "You're next in line."

I can recall yelling and screaming, "I'm pregnant and bleeding, do you even care?!" At this point, I went online and found a customer complaint number and called it. I spoke with a guy who was very helpful and sympathetic to my situation. He told me to give him five minutes. Within the next five minutes, my name was being called back to get treatment. By this time, my husband had left, and one of my aunts was there. She and I walked back to the exam room. The doctors began an ultrasound and I heard my baby's heartbeat. It was beating so loudly as if she was fighting for her life. I asked the doctors if this was normal, and they said no, her heart was a little weak and rapid. They suggested bedrest and for me to follow up with my primary OBGYN to get assistance with my hormonal levels. The next day, I went to my OBGYN to follow up with the news from the emergency room visit only for him to suggest not giving me the hormonal treatment and just to do the bed rest. I pleaded with him to change his mind; however, he assured me I would be fine. This news did not sit well with me as I knew in my heart something was wrong.

Two weeks later, I went back for a checkup only for my baby's heartbeat to be very faint. My doctor looked at me with a look of concern on his face and said, "You were right, let's start you on the hormonal treatment." I looked at him in a very disgusted manner. I was angry as I felt he was part of the reason my baby was fighting for her life. I proceeded with the treatment, and my grandmother asked me to come and stay with her for a few months so she could assist me with my pregnancy. I was happy to oblige as I loved being surrounded by her love and care. Two nights into my stay at my grandmother's house, staying in my old room, I began to go through my old clothes and pulled out the box of sandals my aunt had purchased for me at sixteen before her passing. I began to cry and ask her to please tell God to let my baby live. I closed the box and got into bed.

Around four o'clock in the morning, I felt the room become ice cold and saw a bright light coming from the ceiling of the room. As I got up to investigate what was happening, I saw a lady dressed in all white with long flowing hair. She turned around and looked at me. It was my aunt that had passed away when I was sixteen. I looked at her and said, "Auntie, you heard my prayer." I was excited and I showed her my belly and told her about the baby. She looked at me and smiled, but suddenly her smile turned into sadness. She then took her eyes off me, looking away. I said to her "Auntie, is everything ok?" She looked back at me and extended her arms towards my stomach with tears in her eyes, shaking her head no. I kept asking her "Why are you here?" Pleading with her not to take my baby. I knew at that moment my baby had given up her fight. I felt warmness throughout my stomach and pain in my heart as I knew my journey to motherhood had ended.

I jumped out the bed and ran into my mother's room yelling, "The baby's gone, Auntie came and took the baby!" My mother looked at me very confused saying "Go back to bed, you're just having a bad dream." I told her no, it was real, and the baby was gone. She looked at me and said, "Let's just go to the doctor once it opens." These next three hours seemed to be the longest ever. Finally, we got to the doctor's office, and he confirmed that my baby had passed.

I was devastated, angry, sad, and lifeless. It was as if I had departed as well. I remember the doctors asking me questions about the next steps, but I was mentally checked out. Once I regained my composure, I decided to be placed under anesthesia to have the baby removed. There was no way my first experience of pushing my baby out was going to happen this way. Once I had made the decision, I had to wait two weeks before the procedure. These were two of the hardest weeks to endure. Walking around with a dead fetus in my belly. I no longer felt the movement of my baby. Once the day came for surgery, my husband would yet again let me down. He advised me that he would not be a part of this. My sister and mother stepped in and took me. I was prepped and wheeled into surgery. I was given anesthesia with a five-minute countdown and was out.

An hour into my procedure I remember waking up and seeing the doctors walking around, my legs in the air strapped to metal lifts. I then looked to the left of me and saw a metal surgical pan with the fetus of my baby on it. I began to look closer at it and I saw one of her arms separated from her body. I screamed, "What did you do to my baby?!" The doctors and nurse staff heard me and noticed that I had woken up they proceeded to give me more sedatives to place me back under. After recovery, I noticed my grieving turned into my eagerness to try again as my doctor told me it would be a good idea to do so during this time. I told my husband, and he assured me that he was on board with the process; however, for the next seven months, he would not touch me nor was there any intimacy. This is when I fell back into losing myself again and not feeling worthy or attractive. I tried so many times to get my husband to see me by dressing up sexy and making him his favorite meals, setting the mood with candles and soft music. As he walked into the room, he turned on the lights, pushed past me, and said "Not now." I felt so low at that moment that I went to the bedroom and cried myself to sleep.

The next morning, we had a big argument about him not being there for me and the lack of intimacy. This then turned into a heated moment of passion which caused me to become pregnant yet again. This time I was so excited and sad at the same time. I noticed my marriage wasn't what I had expected, and that my husband was entertaining several conversations with other women. I confronted him about it. He didn't deny it but admitted to the fact he didn't cheat. Everything was there in black and white, and the lack of intimacy was a factor. In that setting, I no longer cared about the state of our marriage as my child was my priority. I was six weeks into my pregnancy when I noticed a burning feeling in my lower back and saw spotting again. I was yet again experiencing complications in another pregnancy. I went to my doctor only to be told it was implantation bleeding and I would be fine. This was when I decided to get a second opinion. At this appointment, the doctor confirmed my pregnancy but could not find the baby on the ultrasound. I went into panic mode. The doctor asked if she could press on my stomach. I said yes and as she pressed to the left; I felt the most horrific pain imaginable. She asked if I was ok. I said "No." She then asked me to sit up as I got up blood began to pour out of me. That's when my doctor yelled out for help.

She told me I was experiencing an ectopic pregnancy and I needed to get to the hospital as soon as possible. She made arrangements for me to get into the operating room and asked my husband to take me across the street for assistance. It was this moment that would change our marriage forever. My husband looked at me and the doctor and stated that he had to get to work. My doctor told him how serious this was and that she would give his manager documentation on why he needed to miss work. As soon as the doctor left the room to provide this information, he walked out of the room, leaving me alone, saying "Call your mom and figure it out." I was abandoned again, this time by my partner, leaving my mother and sister to be there with me.

Once I got to the hospital, I was told I had to wait four hours before I could get the surgery because the wait for my family to arrive allowed someone else into the operating room. Once in surgery, it was a seven-and-a-half-hour process resulting in my left fallopian tube to rupture and my baby not surviving. After waking up again from a procedure to remove a pregnancy, I could not feel anything past the lower half of my body. I was unable to walk on my own nor was I able to able to use my bladder function without the assistance of a catheter. For four months, I went through rehab to regain my ability to walk and bladder function.

I was doing this all alone without the support of my husband. I was done. Done with the ideas of motherhood and marriage. I felt as if I was not deserving. But in these events, I had not grieved. I was losing baby after baby, and my marriage was proven to be over. During my recovery, I finally found the ability to get help with my grieving as well as finding the strength to finally end my marriage. It was not easy to do but it was necessary as this final stage of my marriage took a turn for the worse - mentally, physically, and emotionally. Regaining my strength, loving myself, and letting go allowed my pain to become my power.

Always know that grief is not a linear process, and healing takes time. Focus on taking small steps each day and be patient with yourself. Allow yourself to experience both good and bad days without judgment. Seek professional help if needed. Practice self-compassion. Be kind and gentle with yourself as you grieve. It's natural to experience a range of emotions including anger, guilt, or confusion. Remember that it's okay to feel these emotions and that healing is a personal and unique process. Everyone's experience with grief is different, and there is no right or wrong way to grieve. It's important to find what works best for you and to allow yourself the time and space to go through your healing.

CHAPTER 3

Finding Your Purpose

Understanding Your Strengths and Gifts

Finding your purpose can be a lifelong journey filled with self-discovery and introspection. It's a quest to uncover the unique combination of talent, what you are passionate about, and the values that define who you are and what you want to contribute to the world. To start this journey, it's important to reflect on your interests and what brings you joy. What activities are you excited to explore? What topics or issues ignite a fire within you? Exploring your ideas can provide clues to your purpose. Additionally, examining your values and beliefs can help guide you toward your purpose. What principles do you hold close to your heart? What causes or activities align with your core values? Understanding what you stand for can give you a sense of direction and purpose. Finding your purpose also requires self-reflection and self-analysis.

Take the time to understand your strengths and weaknesses, as well as your unique perspectives and experiences. Reflecting on your past accomplishments and moments of fulfillment can provide insights into what brings you a sense of purpose. It's important to remember that finding your purpose is not a linear process. It may involve trial and error, taking risks, and exploring different paths. Embrace the journey and allow yourself to evolve and grow along the way. Ultimately, your purpose is not something that can be found outside of yourself. It resides within you, waiting to be discovered and nurtured. Embracing your passions, values, and strengths will lead you closer to living a life of purpose and fulfillment. So, embark on the journey, be open to new experiences, and trust that your purpose will reveal itself when the time is right. In developing my purpose, my main target was what makes me happy and gives me a sense of accomplishment. For me, it was trusting myself more, letting go of what others may think, and stepping into my calling. Allowing my faith to guide me in listening to God and embracing my spiritual gifts. My passion for helping others has always given me the feeling that I was doing something good by assisting others.

My spiritual gifts of prophecy and healing were given to me at a very early age. I can recall several times in my childhood when I would see things happening in my dreams come to fruition. I could touch someone's hand and see things in their past and future. This made me a bit apprehensive to shake hands at times. It wasn't until I was an adult that I prayed for an understanding of how to tap into my gifts and embrace them. I can remember God giving me insight into how I was to use my gifts. He told me I was called to fulfill a purpose that would lead many people to him, help others find their purpose, and strengthen their faith. During the 2020 pandemic, I felt the strongest pull to use my gifts to help others during this time. I'm going to tell you, it was not easy. As a Christian and being involved in the church house for years, stepping into my ability to be insightful was something I feared would not be accepted; however, I tapped into my faith and the Bible, reciting the Bible verse Ephesians 4:24 "And to put on the new self, created after the likeness of God in true righteousness and holiness." This reminded me that I was created in his image and that we as humans are in the image of God in our moral, spiritual, and intellectual nature.

Once I let go of the fear of judgment, I embraced my calling and began my journey. I started my online business and crafted a podcast that, on the very first episode, raked in over 700 views. I knew at that moment I was reaching people to help them find the strength, healing, and path to discover their purposes. This platform would become a weekly live stream where people would come to gain knowledge of different topics and insights. I have connected with so many people from all over the world. This allowed many doors of opportunity to open for success but also created new connections. During the pandemic, I ran across someone who was doing live streams on Facebook as well. His messages were so captivating and relatable. He talked about his health battles, how he struggled with his illness, and how he had beaten it. I wrote him a message letting him know how much his story resonated with me as I also had health challenges in the past. We talked about how we overcame our battles and how we moved forward with life. He talked about going back to work and embracing his calling as a healthcare provider. We quickly formed a friendship. Our passion for helping others became our connection (as well as a passion for cooking). Over the years we would discuss so many ways we wanted to help others and create ways to execute our plans. He would always encourage me to keep going and make sure to tune into my podcast. I was very appreciative of our friendship.

In March of 2022, he was hit again, battling the illness as it had come back. He reached out to me, and we prayed together and found ways of spiritual healing. I would send him daily prayers and holistic methods of healing. By the summer of 2022, he had regained his health yet again. He was happy and started living his life, creating new memories, traveling, and connecting more with his family. He went back to work, and he started back on his own podcast. He was nominated for several awards, winning each one. Things were finally going back to normal as we expected; however, the next year 2023 would bring back the illness yet again. As things progressed for me, I closed on my very first home and my friend was unable to celebrate this achievement with me. Our daily prayers continued, and he kept me updated on his recovery. I remember him not being able to go anywhere for months. We found other ways to keep our friendship going by exchanging watchlist movies, TV shows, and documentaries. In June of 2023, he was well enough to go out. I remember him saying to me that he wanted to come by to see my new house.

He called me and said, "I know how much you love ice cream, and I want to bring your favorite flavor." I told him he didn't have to. Several hours had passed by, and I began to worry.

I called him and asked, "Is everything ok?"

He said, "Yes, and open the door." Once I opened the door, he handed me the ice cream. I smiled and was so appreciative.

I asked him, "What took you so long to get here?"

He responded, "Because I went to five different stores to find your favorite flavor." I hugged him and grabbed two bowls so we could enjoy the ice cream together. He took off his jacket, and I noticed his small frame and how frail he was. He looked at me and said, "I know right." I looked back at him and said it was ok and not to worry, that God was going to make him better again. We both began to cry and pray together. Suddenly, I noticed him becoming very weak and tired. He said he was leaving to go home, but my spiritual intuition told me he needed to stay. I told him to go upstairs to my guest room and lie down until he got his strength back. He did and left the following morning. The next few months he would share his health updates with me, and we would continue our daily prayers. On November 27, 2023, he reached out to me for a call just to gain some spiritual advice. We talked about how important his faith was and how I knew in my heart that God was going to make things better like before. Twenty minutes into the call I heard the angels and God tell me not to say anything else. They kept telling me that something was going to happen on Friday. I told him there was something about Friday and that we should talk on Friday to see how things go. Once I ended the call, a very sad feeling overtook my emotions, and I knew at that moment that this time would be different.

A few days went by, and Friday came, and I had no call or text from him. I sent a message just to check on him, but no response. I figured maybe he was feeling well or was back in the hospital. It wasn't until a few days later that a mutual friend of ours made a Facebook post announcing his passing. I looked at the post and saw that he had passed away on the Friday we were supposed to talk. I felt so empty inside as I had lost yet another person who was a great friend and a great person to others. His heart was so genuine and giving. Adding my spiritual insight into our friendship was always something I felt I could help him with. But this time I knew that things would not go the way we hoped. How was I to tell someone that they were not going to make it through? I couldn't. I felt like I had let him down. I wanted so badly to heal him. I wanted him to experience more life experiences, become a husband, have children, and continue to be the best doctor ever. Not a day goes by that I don't think of him and his contagious smile.

My spiritual calling sometimes provides me with heartbreak. I also question myself on how I can change things and outcomes. Sometimes my gift is just meant to offer support in situations of transition. God has a plan for each and every one of us. Being spiritual has its advantages and disadvantages; however, I wouldn't trade it at all. I am thankful for all that God has given me and I will continue to uplift and support others spiritually. This unfortunate experience has shaped my ability to be stronger and led me to have an understanding that in some cases I must know that God is in control and allow God to take the lead.

Know that your purpose may evolve and change over time, and you may not be able to change everything. Embrace the growth and adaptation that comes with it. Be open to new opportunities, experiences, and insights that may expand or refine your sense of purpose. Embracing growth allows you to continue aligning your life with your evolving purpose. Remember, embracing your purpose is a personal journey. It is unique to you and may look different from others. Trust yourself, be patient with the process, and allow your purpose to unfold naturally. Embracing your purpose brings a sense of fulfillment, joy, and alignment to your life, allowing you to make a positive impact on yourself and the world around you. Overall, self-reflection provides the time and space for introspection and self-discovery. It helps you dive deep into your values, passions, strengths, and desires, allowing you to uncover the essence of your purpose. By gaining clarity through self-reflection, you can align your life with what truly matters to you and create a sense of fulfillment and meaning. Living a purpose-driven life allows us to live authentically with a sense of fulfillment and joy. It gives us a sense of meaning and satisfaction as we make a positive impact on ourselves and those around us. Ultimately, purpose is about finding and embracing what brings us alive and using our unique gifts and talents to contribute to the greater good.

How to Find Your Purpose

Some tips I find helpful when it comes to finding your purpose. Remember these six important things:

1. **It's a personal journey:** Your purpose is exclusive to you. It's not something that can be defined by societal expectations or comparisons to others. No one is the same as we are all unique. Embrace the fact that your purpose may be different from those around you and focus on discovering what truly brings you completion.

2. **It takes time:** Finding your purpose is not an overnight process. It requires patience, self-reflection, and searching. Be open to trying new things, giving life to something you are passionate about, and embracing unforeseen

opportunities along the way. Obstacles will arise when you are evolving into your purpose.

3. **It may develop:** Your purpose may change and evolve as you grow and experience different stages of life. What may have resonated with you in the past may not necessarily be the same in the future. Learn to let go of what didn't work out and open your mind to tapping into new ideas!

4. **It's not just about your career:** While your purpose can certainly be associated with your career, it's important to remember that purpose extends beyond a job. It encompasses all aspects of your life including relationships, personal growth, and making a positive impact in the world.

5. **It's about fulfillment, not external validation:** Your purpose should bring you a sense of fulfillment and inner satisfaction rather than seeking validation from others. Focus on what truly brings you joy and aligns with your values rather than chasing external markers of success or approval.

6. **It's okay to seek guidance:** Finding your purpose can sometimes feel overwhelming, and it's perfectly fine to seek guidance from mentors, coaches, or trusted friends and family members. They can offer support, provide different perspectives, and help you navigate through the process. Remember, finding your purpose is a continuous journey of self-discovery. Embrace the process, stay open-minded, and trust in yourself to uncover a purpose that brings meaning and fulfillment to your life.

CHAPTER 4

Breaking Generational Cycles

How I Broke My Generational Cycle

Generational cycles can cause a lot of dynamics in your life whether positive or negative. Breaking generational cycles can be a process of consciously and intentionally stopping the negative patterns or behaviors that have been passed down from one generation to another within a family or community.

Often these cycles can manifest in various ways such as financial, addiction, abuse, or unhealthy relationship patterns. What I have learned in my life is that these cycles only repeat if you are not willing to make the necessary changes. Once we give life to something, it only continues to manifest and create patterns.

In my journey to peel off my layer of negative generational cycles, I had to realize that I was in control of my thoughts and actions. That if I wanted things to change it would have to start within me. I noticed that there were some cycles in my family history that I was repeating. The main course of my pattern was my cycle of relationships. Growing up I never saw what a healthy or successful relationship looked like. Not understanding how a man was supposed to love a woman and a woman love a man. How to receive proper love or embrace an organic flow of love. I found myself forcing love and accepting relationships I knew wouldn't work out. I had developed in my mind that I could fix him, change him, or mold him into the person I hoped he would be. This would allow me to show my family that I could have a successful relationship even if it jeopardized my happiness. So many times I felt myself slipping back into familiar situations. I was pouring so much into my relationships only to have my cup empty. I sat back and watched someone else grow while I was still planted, waiting for someone to water me for my moment of growth, not understanding at that moment I was in control of my own happiness.

I remember, after my divorce, leaving myself out. Doubting myself and my self-worth. This was one time in my life when I felt as if I had failed. I had so many sleepless nights beating myself up about why it failed, what I did wrong, and why I was not good enough. However, what I failed to realize was I had married someone who was already broken, and I was trying to fix him as if he were a build-a-bear project. But the only thing I couldn't add was a heart. You can love a person unconditionally by giving them the best of you and still receive the bare minimum. I found myself slipping into depression as I thought everything was falling apart. Trying to once again after my divorce forcing relationships to happen because I wanted someone to love me and see my worth. Once I let go of my fear of being alone and struggle with self-worth. God told me to isolate myself, to work on my healing, and personal growth. I took heed to his message and remained celibate. I started my businesses and worked on my fitness, relationship with God, and self-confidence. I felt so strong in my journey as if I had finally figured out how to love myself. After two years of growing to become a better version of myself, my grandmother became ill and later passed away. She told me before she passed that she was proud of me and that I would soon find someone to love me and see the value and God in me. She told me my time was coming. I thanked her for her words of motivation, hugged her, and felt a feeling so strong over me as if everything I had prayed for was finally starting to feel right. Two weeks after my talk with my grandmother she passed away. I felt broken all over again, but I had peace knowing that she was no longer hurting. She was ready to leave. She told me that she had seen God, and he was taking her home.

On the day we had her service, I posted a photo on my Facebook page of me standing next to her photo with the caption "She's always by my side." I had such a pouring of support on my post. I recall my mother reaching out to me saying, "Hey, this guy that your grandmother was a fan of commented on your post." I was like, ok? She then went on to say that she remembered my grandmother telling her that someone in our family was going to meet him. I told her that was great, and she asked, "Are you going to say anything back?"

I told her, "Not really," as I didn't even know who this man was. Apparently, he and I had been friends on Facebook for about eight years without ever interacting. After a moment of thought, I went ahead and messaged him with a "Thank you."

Not even five minutes later, he said, "You're welcome, and thank you for reaching out. Do you or your family needed anything?"

I replied, "No, and thank you." He then responded, asking if we could exchange numbers and stay in touch with each other. He gave me his number, and I replied with mine. A few minutes later he called, and we talked for almost two hours about life and how much we had in common. Our connection was divinely ordained. But what made it special was the genuine connection. His celebrity status never affected my love for him, as I didn't even know his status. I knew his heart. They say you learn things in every relationship; in this one, I learned that broken hearts can heal. I felt that I could completely let my guard down and allow love to come in. He opened up to me about a lot of things from his past, and we connected more by spiritually helping each other release things that were no longer a part of our journey. We would ground together, and spend nights immersed in conversation. I knew in my heart that this was it. I saw something in him that the world didn't see. His venerability, the mere shyness, his comedic side. The way he would make me laugh and smile; I felt safe placing my heart in his hands. Were things finally going in the right direction? Did I crack the code? Was I actually in love this time, organically?

Just as things were looking good, he began to become distant, and our communication was very different. I wasn't getting the best of him anymore. That's when I turned into a detective. You know, once you go looking for something, you're going to find it. I found out that he was still entangled in a "situationship" with his so-called ex. Once I confronted him with my findings, he told me that he had to play a role with her because they were bonded together in multiple business deals. I was devastated, broken, and confused. I was finally happy, but everything was not what it seemed to be. He was deceiving my heart. As much as I wanted to stay, I knew I had to let go. It hurt so much as I believed I had finally met my purpose partner and I had accomplished the feeling of being in love.

For the next three months, I put my heart on ice. I was determined not to go through another failed relationship. It was me for me, and this time I was taking control. But was I? The feeling of letting go of this man was starting to get the best of me. During those three months, he would reach out to me several times asking me to come back; however, I didn't responded. I wanted so badly to move on, but my heart was with him. I decided to reach out. He invited me to dinner where we talked. He told me he wanted to give us another try, and this time he was going to be as transparent as possible. He showed me documentation and emails stating he was cutting all ties with his ex. He asked me if I would consider marriage and move in with him. I was so excited to hear this, and I agreed. A week later I began transitioning myself to living with him. We spent the next three months spending every night together. He would have his driver and security team take me on shopping trips. Walking around with bodyguards and having personal shoppers was becoming my life. Don't get me wrong, it was truly an experience, but I was missing being able to go to the store alone or just doing the normal things I used to enjoy without staff around.

One night I decided to go back to my house to check on things as I had been away for about three months. I called and told him I was going to stay the night and come back in the morning. I did some chores, relaxed, and got ready for bed. At about 2 AM the next day he called me to come back in a panic. I got in my car and drove back there. As I pulled up, the energy was different, and there was a car in the driveway that I had never seen before. I pulled around to the back, texted him I was there, and went up the stairs. Once I got to the top, I heard laughter and a female voice. I went to open the door but it was locked. I tapped on the door for him to open it.

Once I tapped, I heard the female say, "Who's at your door?" She then attempted to open it only to be restrained by him. She broke loose and began to run towards the door asking, "Who is she?" I could hear her saying she was going to beat me up. I could see her through the window, trying to break free from him to get to me. I stood there and began to laugh. It was funny to me because she wasn't going to beat me up. This was not something she would succeed at. Secondly, why was she even there? Lastly, why would he call me over there, and what was really going on? In that setting, I felt it was a complete setup.

I could hear him yelling out "Don't leave baby, I'm trying to get her out of my house." I was confused, and I left. Several times he called my phone, asking me to come back, stating that the other woman had popped up. But why now? On the one day I left his house out of three months. This time I was completely done as he had played me to my face one too many times.

I knew it was wrong; I was not supposed to keep going back. I was yet again repeating cycles that I tried so hard to break. This was a true wake-up call to remain centered on my journey. To allow time for the proper relationship to come along. Sometimes the enemy comes in and distracts you in moments of healing, presenting you with things you feel are what you desire. It's called temptation. I'm still trusting the process and allowing God to order my steps in the direction he has for me. Remind yourself that God will not send you anything of confusion nor distract you to throw you off course. Remain focused on breaking the generational cycles in your family history. These steps outlined in the next section will guide you in your process. Each day you are one step closer to getting all that belongs to you.

Steps to Breaking Generational Cycles

To break generational cycles, several steps can be taken:

1. **Awareness and acknowledgment:** Recognize and acknowledge the existence of the generational cycles within your family or community. Understand how these cycles have affected your life and the lives of those around you.

2. **Education and self-reflection:** Learn about the root causes and dynamics behind the generational cycles. This may involve reading books, attending workshops, or seeking therapy. Engage in self-reflection to understand your own beliefs, values, and behaviors that may contribute to the cycle.

3. **Set new goals and values:** Define your vision for a different future. Identify the values and goals that you want to prioritize and instill in the next generation. This may include concepts like education, financial stability, healthy relationships, and personal growth.

4. **Seek support and build a network:** Surround yourself

with people who support your desire to break the generational cycle. This network can include friends, family members, mentors, or support groups. Share your goals and challenges with them and seek their guidance and encouragement.

5. **Break the silence and open communication**: Break the silence surrounding the generational cycle by openly discussing it with your family or community. Encourage open and honest communication about the challenges and experiences faced by each generation. This can help in understanding the underlying issues and finding solutions together.

6. **Embrace self-care and well-being**: Take care of your physical, mental, and emotional well-being. Break the cycle of neglect or self-destructive behaviors by prioritizing self-care and seeking professional help if needed. By taking care of yourself, you set an example for future generations.

7. **Empower the next generation**: Teach the younger generation about the importance of breaking generational cycles. Provide them with the necessary tools, resources, and support to make better choices and create a different future. Encourage their dreams, aspirations, and personal growth.

Breaking generational cycles is a gradual and ongoing process that requires commitment, resilience, and patience. It involves making conscious choices and taking proactive steps to create a positive change for yourself and future generations.

CHAPTER 5

Setting Boundaries: Building Healthy Relationships

Learning to Set Boundaries

Boundaries are essential for establishing and maintaining healthy relationships. They serve as guidelines that define acceptable behavior and protect our physical, emotional, and mental well-being. In this chapter, we will explore the importance of setting boundaries, how to recognize when boundaries are needed, and learn practical strategies for establishing and enforcing them effectively.

Setting boundaries is an ongoing process that requires self-awareness, effective communication, and assertiveness. By establishing and enforcing boundaries, we can create healthier relationships, protect our well-being, and foster mutual respect and understanding. Remember, setting boundaries is not selfish, but essential for personal growth and maintaining healthy connections with others.

Putting boundaries in place can sometimes be a little difficult, especially when you have a giving heart. Having a pure heart was always something that I felt people would take advantage of. In my journey to peel off my layer of enforcing boundaries, I had to understand that saying no was not a bad thing, nor was it selfish. It was me taking control of who had access to me and putting limits on what I was no longer going to deal with. When you start to limit the amount of access people have to you, that's when you start to see their true intentions. My biggest challenge with setting boundaries was my trust in others. Mainly, in my friendships. I have always been the friend who takes loyalty seriously and values my relationships with my friends. One person, in particular, was someone who I looked at not only as a friend but as family. I met this person during my healing process of understanding who I was spiritually, and when I was releasing my hurt. This person helped me to identify how to enforce my boundaries with family and friends. We connected spirituality, and we both had a passion for helping others. It was a great match between two influencers with a purpose.

However, from my perspective, I noticed moments of jealousy, especially once I entered my last relationship. This person would say things like, "I only date men of power or men who are financially established." This person even went to the extreme to say that they wanted my relationship to fail. I was totally taken aback as this was someone I called my best friend. They even said to me that I didn't deserve this type of happiness. I told them that I didn't appreciate that type of energy or how that made me feel. This was when they began to gaslight me, manipulating me into questioning my own perception of reality. I trusted this person so much that I overshared a lot of my relationship and struggles with them, not understanding that I was giving them too much freedom within my personal boundaries. Too much access to my struggles and vulnerability. I was giving them the necessary tools to use to manipulate me.

Did I take heed of this at that moment? No. Why? I felt I had built a solid friendship of over five years with this person and allowed myself to depend on their guidance and feedback. As I continued through the friendship, I would continue to be a supportive friend mentally, spiritually, and financially. I would help them with advice on whatever they were going through without judgment or negativity, thinking this would show them how to extend grace and be a better friend. But what I kept getting back in return was being used and negative feedback. I remember going to God and asking him to show me if this person was genuine. I remember asking God to humble this person to show them how to become a better friend. A few months after my prayers and my going to God, this person came to me in desperate need of help. They were going through a lot of relationship drama, mental struggles with anxiety, and a huge financial burden. I can recall several times this person reached out to me for financial assistance.

Whether it was money for a bill or money for food, as a friend watching one of my friends go through a huge struggle, especially financially, I did not want to turn my back on them. I continued assisting, lending an amount of almost over $3,000. It was never me giving them a time limit on when to pay me back as I thought this person was going through such a huge struggle. During one of the happiest moments in my life when I became a new homeowner, I told this person of my happiness. Instead of responding with kindness, they were saying things like "Why would you buy a house?" "You need to help me." Even to the point of saying "If you're buying a house that means you have good credit, right?" Then they went on to say, "You need to take out an almost $50,000 loan and give me the money to help get me out of debt." At this point, I was literally over it.

Because of this fake friendship and being used by someone who I truly respected and valued the friendship of, I started pulling back from my communications and focused on my home closing and romantic relationship. I closed on my home and continued to work on myself and my business. My Facebook livestream was taking off, and I was guiding others to become better versions of themselves. As I was guiding others, I had to practice what I was preaching. I started evaluating my friendship with this person, and I prayed about it. If it was for me, it would present a better alignment of an organic connection. During this time, I would keep my conversations short and try to have purposeful conversations. A month later, I can recall seeing this person on social media posting lavish trips and designer apparel. This didn't look like someone who was having financial hardships. I kept my thoughts to myself and continued to focus on myself. Two days later, I was out of town on business, and I got a frantic call from this person stating they were in dire need of help financially.

They asked if I could send them $600. I was like, "For what?" They replied that they needed it to pay back a friend they had borrowed money from. I was confused and upset. How could you ask someone for money to pay back someone else when you owed me money? But what did I do? I tried to assist. Yes, I did. Once again, I was trying to show them how big my heart was, as if I had something to prove or teach them. I didn't feel at that moment as if I was being weak or a pushover. It was about testing this friendship one last time. I told them to give me an hour or so to get through my meeting and see what I could do. They agreed. I felt like if they trusted me to do what I always did, then they could wait. About two hours later, I reached out to assist, only to receive a text message about how bad of a friend I was and not to ever worry about helping them again. I responded back with, "I never said no, I simply said let me see what I can do."

This was a test they failed but an awakening for me to understand I had given all I had to give in this friendship. Not even an hour later, I was removed from their social media accounts and blocked on their phone. I was talked about on their social media accounts, they told many lies to mutual friends, and they really tried to assassinate my character. All this was simply because I did not move or jump when they wanted me to. I was enforcing my boundaries. They flipped the narrative and told people that I was the one who they were helping financially. However, the part that was so appalling was that I never said anything about them or the situation at hand. I remained silent and let them say what they wanted as I took the high road and let God expose them.

Was I mad or hurt? No, I wasn't as I had finally enforced my boundaries and allowed God to remove anyone that was no longer a part of my journey. I learned several lessons in this friendship. I learned to stand strong in what I felt, to not allow anyone to take advantage of my kindness, and to give closure to people who are not in the friendship or relationship to enhance my life. Know that it's ok to walk away. Learn to make sure people respect your nos. Stand strong in your power, and do not allow anyone to take you for granted. Remember, in life, you will be sent destiny helpers along the way, and everyone who helps you through hard times or moments in your life where you were struggling with something the helpers are not always meant to stay. Give closure properly and walk away gracefully. Not everything deserves addressing. Especially when they show the world exactly who the weakest link is by taking issues to others instead of the person that they have the issue with.

How to Set Boundaries With Friends

Enforcing boundaries with a friend is an important aspect of maintaining a healthy and respectful relationship. Here are a few steps I've learned that you can take to enforce boundaries with a friend:

1. **Reflect on your boundaries:** Before addressing the issue with your friend, take some time to reflect on your own boundaries. Identify what is acceptable and what is not in your friendship.

2. **Communicate openly:** Schedule a time to talk to your friend in a calm and non-confrontational manner. Clearly express your concerns and the specific boundaries that you feel are being crossed.

3. **Be assertive:** When discussing an issue, it's important to be assertive and confident in expressing your needs and boundaries. Use "I" statements to avoid sounding accusatory and focus on how their actions make you feel.

4. **Set clear consequences:** Let your friend know what the consequences will be if they continue to disregard your boundaries. This could include spending less time together, taking a break from the friendship, or even ending the friendship if necessary.

5. **Seek support if needed:** If your friend continues to disregard your boundaries or if the situation becomes emotionally draining, it may be helpful to seek support from a trusted friend or a counselor who can provide guidance and perspective.

Remember, enforcing boundaries is not about being mean or controlling but about ensuring that your needs and feelings are respected in the friendship.

How to Set Boundaries With Significant Others, Family, or Work

When enforcing boundaries in relation to other relationships like with family, work colleagues, or a partner. enforcing boundaries becomes an important aspect of maintaining healthy relationships and personal well-being. Here are some steps I feel you can take to enforce boundaries effectively:

1. **Identify your boundaries:** Take the time to reflect on your values, needs, and limits. Understand what behaviors or actions are acceptable or unacceptable to you in different areas of your life such as work, relationships, and personal space.

2. **Communicate your boundaries clearly:** Clearly express

your boundaries to others. Use "I" statements to express how certain behaviors or actions make you feel and why you need those boundaries in place. Be assertive, firm, and confident when communicating your boundaries.

3. **Be consistent:** Consistently reinforce your boundaries by following through with the consequences you have established. This shows others that you are serious about maintaining your boundaries and helps establish a sense of respect.

4. **Practice self-care:** Prioritize self-care to ensure that you have the energy and emotional capacity to enforce your boundaries. Take care of your physical, mental, and emotional well-being, as this will help you stay strong and confident in maintaining your boundaries.

5. **Seek support:** Surround yourself with supportive people who respect your boundaries. Share your experiences and challenges with trusted friends, family, or a therapist who can provide guidance and encouragement.

6. **Learn to say no:** Saying no is an essential skill when enforcing boundaries. Practice setting clear limits and saying no when something goes against your boundaries. Remember that it's okay to prioritize your own well-being and say no when necessary.

7. **Reflect and adjust:** Periodically reflect on your boundaries and assess if they are still serving you. As you grow and evolve, your boundaries may need to be adjusted or updated to align with your changing needs and values.

Remember, enforcing boundaries is a continuous process that requires self-awareness, assertiveness, and self-care. It may take time and practice, but with consistency and determination, you can effectively enforce your boundaries and maintain healthier relationships.

CHAPTER 6

Giving Closure

How I Found Closure

Closure is an important concept in various aspects of life including relationships, projects, and personal growth. It refers to the process of finding a resolution or ending, allowing you to move forward and gain a sense of peace and understanding. Providing clear and honest explanations about the situation or decision that led to the need for closure. This can include expressing your thoughts, feelings, and reasons behind the decision. Actively listening and acknowledging their perspective can help in providing closure. Discussing possible resolutions or next steps that can help both parties move forward. This may involve making compromises, finding mutual agreements, or making plans for the future.

On my journey to peel off my layer of giving closure, I had to identify what or who needed to receive the closure from me. I created a list of people who needed closure. I identified my boundaries, poured into myself, and understood how to stand in my power. I was in a position to shorten my list as I had removed a toxic one-sided friendship. I was determined not to compromise my happiness again, nor was I going to be anyone's reoccurring, revolving door. I was closing the door to everything that no longer deserved a place in my life. I had let go of my insecurities, fear of being alone, fake friends, failed relationships, and heartbreak. I realized, as I was peeling off each layer, that I was becoming lighter. The load I had carried for so long was slowly falling to my feet. I am now more aware of my boundaries.

Ending my attachments and giving closure was what I needed. Walking away from my toxic relationship and understanding not to be someone's "pick me." I had been spending too much time on layaway. I realized I was in a layaway relationship, the kind where they take you off the market but place you in the back room until they are ready to invest in you. I wasted time waiting for him to see just how special I was. Waiting for my moment with him. I was tired of being in the background. I wanted to showcase my relationship and let everyone know just how happy I was.

For two years, I dedicated my life to this person, being his biggest support, encouraging him, and letting him know daily just how special he was to me and how much I loved him. All this only to have, what I thought was so beautiful and special, be something that would fade in the wind, blowing away like fire to a wick. The sweet aroma left the room once the fire was out. I wanted so badly for this to work. I knew his heart, his weakness. I mastered how to make him feel better when times were tough, even when I was hurting. I would put my feelings on hold to be what he needed me to be in his moments of pain and depression. I recall one day I was sick with a low fever and could barely get out of bed when he asked me to come over. I told him how bad I was feeling, and that I probably wouldn't make it. He became very upset and challenged my love for him by telling me I didn't care and that he was slipping back into depression. He always had a way of making you feel empathic by gaslighting you. This was always his tactic when he wanted things his way. However, I got out of bed on his promise to help aid me in my sickness and made my way to his home. Once I arrived, he greeted me with a warm embrace and flowers. I went to his room, lay down, and attempted to get some sleep. Not even ten minutes later, he came into the room, ordering me to do things he needed to get done. Wash his clothes, steaming his shirts, and fixing him a meal. I looked at him like, "You can't be serious right now." I was literally weak and tired from the cold that was taking over my body.

He said to me, "Yes, I need these done, and my assistant is no longer here." I declined to assist and told him how bad I was feeling. But that didn't seem to even concern him. He wanted what he wanted, and he wanted it now. I knew at that moment it was just another setup for him to get what he needed out of me. He knew exactly how to manipulate me.

He knew how big my heart was and how I loved him so much that I would always be there for him. Having little energy and body aches from the cold, my body was so weak and tired. I continued to lie down until he came back into the room with more demands. I reminded him of this promise to take care of me as I thought that was the reason I was there. I then decided I wasn't going to continue going back and forth with him and started to get my things and leave. He became angry and told me to get out of his house. I remained silent and continued to grab my things. That's when he threw my bag at me and grabbed my arm, trying to escort me out. I told him to let go, and that this wasn't necessary. I started to cry as I had never seen this side of him. I was scared and nervous as I had no idea what was going to happen next. I just remember running down the stairs to my car.

Once I got downstairs, he ran right after me. He ran in front of my car door, blocking me from opening it. He grabbed my hand and fell to his knees, crying. Pleading with me to stay and apologizing for his actions. He told me he needed me, and that he would never do anything to hurt me. For me, it was too late. This gave me flashbacks to the ten-year relationship I was in that became abusive. I was still so sick that I remember nearly fainting. He picked me up and took me back upstairs, laid me in the bed, and held me all night. We fell asleep crying together in each other's arms. I woke up the next morning with him next to me, looking at me as if I was the most precious gem he had ever seen.

He took off work that morning, made me some tea, and took care of me for the next two days. On the day that I left, he placed a thousand dollars in my purse and sent me a nice amount of money through Zelle. He told me to use the money in my purse for food and medicine while the Zelle was for his actions the other night. He made promises that he would never act in that manner again, and he promised to always protect me. My mind was so confused, but was I really surprised? There were so many red flags in this relationship. This time, I wasn't dealing with a build-a-bear project. I was dealing with Dr. Jekyll and Mr. Hyde. A true definition of narcissistic behavior. Someone who could really tap into your mind and make your reality seem to appear the total opposite of what you believe or thought. This was menacing and dangerous. Why? Because I was losing myself trying to once again show someone I could be all they needed by settling. By giving up my power once again.

Several other events would occur in this relationship that raised more concern and ultimately my exit. The happy love story I wanted with this man was more of a soap opera with many episodes of drama. I knew this was not what I waited two years for. This couldn't be what the universe sent to me. I felt like I was being punked. I was in a bad dream, waiting for someone to wake me up. This was not my love story. I had to end this stage of my life and give closure to this relationship. I knew this was me repeating generational cycles and not enforcing my boundaries. How could I be so strong in helping others when I was allowing myself to be weak?

I was giving too many people too much access to me. I was allowing them to use and abuse our connections. I wasn't standing up for myself. Giving this relationship closure was easy to do this time around. As I wrote my pros and cons list, the bad outweighed the good. My heart was truly not in agreement with my mind, but I knew it was the right thing to do for me. Once I ended things, he became upset, blocking me on social media and his phone. This was becoming the norm for me when I decided to enforce my boundaries and stand up for myself. I was unbothered as this showed me our true connection, that this was just a phase for him, and he picked back up with his ex of ten years. Yeah, the one still waiting on the ring and her moment. His seat filler, the one that holds the spot on the bench, waiting for her time to be let back into the game. As for me, I gave it all to God, and this time around, I was taking my time. No forced connections or moments of confusion. I'm dedicated to my healing and becoming a better me, working on my mental space, physical health, and spiritual journey. Whatever is meant for me will find its way to me. My focus is now on me.

Understand that walking away doesn't make you a quitter, it makes you a winner. A winner of gaining back your inner happiness and strength. Every one of us has the potential to do amazing things in life and to have the true essence of happiness. Continue to identify your goals, make a plan, and put it into action. Give closure where needed and move forward, knowing that all you ever needed was you. Remember, closure is a personal journey, and the process may differ for each individual and situation. It's important to approach it with patience, empathy, and self-compassion, allowing for personal growth and moving forward. Pray about it, and allow God to guide you to your next level of greatness.

Advice on Gaining Closure

Closure is an important aspect of moving on from a past relationship. Here are some steps I feel may guide you in giving closure to a relationship:

1. **Accept your emotions**: Recognize and accept your feelings about the end of the relationship. It's normal to experience a range of emotions including sadness, anger, and confusion. Allow yourself to feel these emotions and give yourself time to process them.

2. **Reflect on the relationship**: Take time to reflect on the relationship and what you have learned from it. Consider both the positive and negative aspects of the relationship and how it has shaped you as an individual.

3. **Communicate your feelings**: If you feel the need to express your emotions or seek closure, consider having a conversation with your ex-partner. Be honest about your feelings, but also be prepared to listen to their perspective. It's important to approach the conversation with respect and an open mind.

4. **Acceptance and forgiveness**: Accept that the relationship has ended and acknowledge that both you and your ex-partner have made mistakes. Forgiving yourself and your ex-partner can help in the process of closure. Remember, forgiveness is not about condoning the actions, but about letting go of anger and resentment.

5. **Focus on personal growth**: Use this opportunity to focus on yourself and your personal growth. Engage in activities that bring you joy, invest time in your hobbies, and surround yourself with supportive friends and family. This will help you move forward and create a fulfilling life without dwelling on the past.

6. **Seek support if needed**: If you find it difficult to achieve closure on your own, consider seeking support from a therapist, counselor, or support group. They can provide guidance and help you navigate through your emotions.

Remember, closure is a personal journey, and it may take time.

Be patient with yourself and trust that, with time, you will be able to find peace and move on from the relationship.

Other Kinds of Closure

Here are a few ways to give closure in different situations:

1. **Relationship Closure:** When ending a romantic relationship or friendship, it's important to have a conversation to provide closure. Express your feelings honestly and respectfully, allowing both parties to share their thoughts and emotions. This conversation can help bring understanding and acceptance, providing closure for both individuals.

2. **Project Closure:** When completing a project or task, it's helpful to have a clear ending to provide closure. This can include reviewing the accomplishments, reflecting on the challenges faced, and acknowledging the contributions of everyone involved. Celebrating the success and expressing gratitude can help bring closure and a sense of accomplishment.

3. **Personal Closure:** In personal growth or healing processes, closure can be achieved by acknowledging and processing emotions related to past experiences. This might involve journaling, therapy, or other forms of self-reflection. By understanding and accepting the emotions associated with a particular event, closure can be obtained.

CHAPTER 7

How to Find Balance

How to Find Balance

In our daily lives and the fast-paced and demanding world, finding balance has become more important than ever. Balancing various aspects of our lives such as work, relationships, health, and personal growth can be a challenging task. However, with the right mindset and strategies, achieving balance is not only possible but also essential for our overall well-being. In this chapter, we will explore some key tools of balance and discover various ways to help you lead a more harmonious and fulfilling life. Being balanced is essential to maintaining a clear mental space. Being balanced allows for a sense of calm and fulfillment, as it encourages a healthy distribution of time, energy, and attention to different priorities and responsibilities. It involves making conscious choices, setting boundaries, and maintaining a sense of self-awareness and self-care to achieve a well-rounded and purposeful life. My journey to peel off the layer of finding my balance wasn't an easy task. I struggled with making people respect my nos and saying no. It was important to me to remember that finding balance is an ongoing process that requires self-awareness and conscious effort. Be patient with yourself and make proper adjustments as needed to ensure you are living a balanced and fulfilling life.

Here are some tips I found useful that assisted me in remaining balanced:

1. **Prioritize self-care:** Take care of your physical, mental, and emotional health. Make time for activities that bring you joy, relaxation, and rejuvenation.

2. **Establish boundaries:** Learn to say no when you need to and set boundaries with others. This will help you avoid feeling overwhelmed and maintain a healthy work-life balance.

3. **Practice mindfulness:** Be present in the moment and cultivate awareness of your thoughts, feelings, and sensations. Mindfulness can help reduce stress and increase your ability to handle challenges.

4. **Maintain a healthy lifestyle:** Eat nutritious food, exercise regularly, and get enough sleep. These habits contribute to your overall well-being and help you stay balanced.

5. **Seek support:** Reach out to friends, family, or a support network when you need assistance or someone to talk to. Building a strong support system can provide guidance and comfort during challenging times.

6. **Manage stress:** Find healthy ways to manage stress, such as practicing relaxation techniques, engaging in hobbies, or participating in activities that bring you joy.

7. **Set realistic goals**: Break down your goals into manageable steps and prioritize what is most important. This approach will help you avoid feeling overwhelmed and maintain a sense of balance.

8. **Embrace flexibility**: Life is full of unexpected changes and challenges. Being flexible and adaptable can help you navigate these situations with ease and maintain a sense of balance.

Balancing a heavy load in my life would often take a toll on me. I was finding myself becoming lost in my plan, my vision, my dreams. I was adding things to my plate that I knew I wasn't going to finish. Why? Simply because I wasn't trusting the process. I was rushing things. I wanted to do things my way and speed up the plans that God had laid before me. I was in pursuit of the wrong happiness. I wanted to try to do things microwavable. You know ready in 30 seconds. Easy, no preparation needed. However, in life greatness is not obtained by a speedy process, but by hard work and determination. By setting goals, creating an attainable plan, trusting the process, and most importantly believing in God.

My Experience Finding Balance

As a Libra sometimes I was concerned with attaining balance and harmony and trying my best to make others happy. When doing this it compromised my own happiness. Mostly in my relationships. I found myself going above and beyond for others only for them to give me the bare minimum in return. This was mainly because I genuinely wanted to have the feeling of being loved and accepted by a man. I wanted romance, something everlasting, an unbreakable bond. For years I allowed myself to repeat patterns of relationship trauma. I was completely lost at times searching for something that I felt was impossible to obtain. Once I realized that I needed to understand what I wanted, I had to find it within myself first. I had to understand what it was I truly desired, and what it was I was no longer going to accept. The lackluster inability of the men I found myself dealing with was killing me emotionally and mentally.

Finding myself drowning in my own thoughts and tears. However, no one heard me, saw me, or even glanced long enough to see the fire that had once sparked in me burn out faster than a candle in the wind. It was easy to get up every day, apply makeup, and walk out the door, still being broken inside. Using every beauty remedy to fix my face and hair, but still couldn't find enough glue to put back the pieces of my heart. It was like my heart was sinking in quicksand and my only way out was to continue to fight alone. But for how long? How much more was I going to allow myself to fight alone in my relationships? Was it time for me to challenge myself? Yes, it was! In order for me to restore life back into my heart I had to first give it back to the person who created it, God. I had to pray, surrender my life back to him, and ask him for his guidance. As I knew deep down in my heart, he had something so much better for me once I accepted me. For whom he created, and who he loved. God's love is unmatched, unconditional, and surpasses any love that anyone walking this earth can provide. Giving my fragile heart to God gave me a calming feeling, a sense of self-awareness being wrapped up in the arms of the almighty God elevated my soul so much that became whole. It was as if everything that I once felt was broken had finally been put back together. Only this time I was made not to be broken down by anything or anyone else that was sent to distract me from my purpose. Most importantly I was back in balance with my mind, body, and spirit. I had connected back with God and had so much reassurance in what my purpose was. Remember, finding balance is a personal journey, and what works for one person may not work for another. It's essential to explore and discover what practices resonate with you and support your relationship with God.

Additional Tips for Finding Personal Balance

Here are some tips that I found helpful in my removal of peeling off the layers of finding my balance. I pray these tips are helpful in your journey.

1. **Prayer and Meditation**: Engaging in regular prayer and meditation can help individuals connect with their spiritual beliefs and find inner peace. Taking time to reflect and seek guidance from God can provide a sense of balance and clarity in life.

2. **Seeking Guidance from Religious Scriptures**: Many religious texts provide teachings and principles that guide believers in leading a balanced life. Reading and studying these scriptures can provide insight and wisdom on how to navigate challenges and make decisions in line with one's values.

3. **Trusting in God's Plan**: Believing in a higher power can help individuals relinquish control over things they cannot change and trust in God's plan for their lives. This trust

can bring a sense of peace and balance, knowing that there is a greater purpose and a divine order at work.

4. **Practicing Gratitude**: Expressing gratitude for the blessings in life, both big and small, can help maintain a positive outlook and foster a sense of balance and contentment. Recognizing and appreciating God's goodness can bring joy and perspective to daily life.

5. **Embracing Faith-based Values**: Integrating faith-based values, such as compassion, forgiveness, and love, into daily interactions and decision-making can contribute to a balanced and harmonious life. Living in alignment with these values can bring fulfillment and a sense of

The Benefits of Gratitude

Also, remember in your journey to always practice expressing gratitude for the blessings in life. This can help you have a profound impact on individuals with a belief in God. Here's how it can contribute to a sense of balance and contentment:

1. **Shifts Focus**: Expressing gratitude redirects our attention from what may be lacking in our lives to what we already have. It helps us recognize and appreciate the blessings, big and small, that God has bestowed upon us. This shift in focus allows us to view our lives from a more positive perspective, fostering a sense of balance and contentment.

2. **Cultivates Humility**: Gratitude reminds us that the blessings we receive are not solely a result of our efforts but are also gifts from God. It cultivates humility by

acknowledging that we are dependent on a higher power for the goodness in our lives. This humility helps us stay grounded and maintain balance, as it prevents us from becoming overly focused on our own achievements or possessions.

3. **Enhances Mindfulness:** Expressing gratitude encourages us to be present in the moment and fully appreciate the gifts around us. By consciously recognizing and giving thanks for the blessings in our lives, we develop a sense of mindfulness. This mindfulness helps us stay connected to the present moment and find contentment in the here and now, rather than dwelling on past regrets or future worries.

4. **Strengthens Faith:** Gratitude is an expression of trust and faith in God's providence. When we acknowledge and give thanks for the blessings we receive, we affirm our belief that God is actively involved in our lives and cares for us. This strengthens our faith and deepens our sense of connection to a higher power. Having a strong faith foundation contributes to a sense of inner peace, balance, and contentment.

5. **Promotes Generosity and Compassion:** Gratitude inspires a spirit of generosity and compassion towards others. When we recognize the blessings in our lives, we are more likely to share our abundance with others and extend kindness. Acts of generosity and compassion contribute to a sense of balance and contentment by fostering positive relationships and creating a ripple effect of gratitude in our communities.

In summary, expressing gratitude for the blessings in life allows individuals with a belief in God to shift their focus, cultivate humility, enhance mindfulness, strengthen faith, and promote generosity and compassion. These elements contribute to a sense of balance and contentment, as they align our hearts and minds with the goodness and grace of a higher power.

Peeling Off the Layers to Unmask New Beginnings
A Guide On How To Create New Beginnings By Peeling Off
Obstacles In Life

In this captivating and introspective guide and testimony, "Peeling Off The Layers to Unmask New Beginnings," embarks on a journey of peeling off layers of adversity, with a detailed guide on overcoming obstacles in life. This book peels off the layers that blocked Stacey Dori from her true potential. Set against doubt, uncertainty, and personal growth, this book explores the transformative power of embracing vulnerability and shedding the weight of past experiences. With each layer unraveled, a new beginning awaits, filled with possibility, authenticity, and renewed hope. Dive into this thought-provoking narrative and let it inspire you to embark on your own journey towards unmasking the hidden depths within. "Peeling Off The Layer To Unmasking New Beginnings" is a testament to the resilience of the strength Stacey Dori displayed and a reminder that true liberation lies in embracing your power by setting boundaries.

About the Author

Stacey "Dori" Garel is a published author and prophetess. Stacey is originally from Atlanta, GA, she is a certified Event Planner professional. Stacey has been a dedicated expert of events for over 15 years.

Having worked on national conferences, trade shows, and events such as the 2012 DNC for former President Barack Obama and the 2013 and 2019 Super Bowl. Stacey is an art lover, a fantastic cook, and loves music. Her ultimate goal is to always be an inspiration to all she encounters.

Linkedin: www.linkedin.com/StaceyGarel
Facebook: https://www.facebook.com/stacey2qute
Instagram: instagram.com/Iamstaceydori

Website:
https://www.yourspiritualgoddess.com
https://www.giftedadministrativeservices.com/